CORPORATE QUICKSAND

KHURSHED DORDI

notionpress.com

INDIA · SINGAPORE · MALAYSIA

ISBN 979-8-89026-033-8

DISCLAIMER

Every effort has been made for this book to be as complete and accurate as possible.

This book provides information only up to the publishing date. Therefore, this book should be used as a guide, not the ultimate source.

The purpose of this book is to educate. The author and the publisher do not warrant that the information contained in this book is fully complete and shall not be responsible for any errors or omissions. The author and publisher shall have neither liability nor responsibility to any person or entity concerning any loss or damage caused or alleged to be caused directly or indirectly by this book.

CONTENTS

Contents

Contents

INTRODUCTION

Even after spending 10 to 20 years in the professional world, many managers and leaders can still feel that they are stuck in their careers. It can be disheartening if you don't seem to be getting ahead despite all the hard work you've put in over the years. Unfortunately, certain common career roadblocks may be standing in your way. These roadblocks include a lack of recognition for your work, difficulty navigating organizational politics, or insufficient resources to grow.

This book is designed to guide professionals to identify the most common career roadblocks and develop strategies to overcome them. The goal is to be proactive about taking control of your growth and moving forward with your professional development. The following chapters will discuss various related topics, including recognizing when you're stuck, identifying the source of your career stagnation, developing strategies for success, and setting goals that will help you reach new heights professionally.

It is important not to get discouraged if progress isn't happening fast enough. This book will show readers how they can use failure as a source of motivation by learning from mistakes and using them as an opportunity for personal growth. Through self-reflection and analysis of your current situation, this book hopes to empower readers with a renewed sense of purpose and actionable steps they can take toward achieving their career goals.

The advice and insights in this book are meant to provide readers with a roadmap for success, helping you to identify and break through your existing career roadblocks and progress toward your ultimate goals. By the end of this book, you will have a clearer understanding of what's been holding you back and how to move forward in your career with confidence. Let's get started!

PART I

UNDERSTANDING CAREER ROADBLOCKS

01 IDENTIFYING THE MOST COMMON CHALLENGES

Determining your career is often strewn with obstacles and roadblocks, but being cognizant of these issues will assist you in tackling them and ultimately, reaching your goal.

Managers and leaders often face many challenges, some more common than others. One of the most common challenges of managers is striking the right balance between being a coach and an authority figure. Managing employees while providing support, guidance, and motivation can be challenging at times. Furthermore, managing multiple teams or departments simultaneously can test a manager's ability to delegate tasks, provide feedback efficiently and effectively, and maintain order.

Many people have been stuck in their careers for several years and are unsure how to move forward. While some individuals may have progressed over time, they can still face multiple challenges that hold them back from reaching the top of their field.

These challenges vary from person to person, but many professionals face common roadblocks in their career progression. Identifying the core issues preventing you from taking control of your professional growth is the first step toward overcoming these challenges.

Below are some of the most common challenges that managers and leaders face in their careers:

Lack of Opportunities for Advancement

Many positions offer limited or no opportunities to advance, leaving you stagnant and stuck in your current role. This can often be due to organizational structure, budget constraints, or other factors beyond your control.

Most employees want to have access to opportunities for professional development and progress. They aim to improve and expand their skill sets. Additionally, they aspire to fill various positions and rise through the company ranks. If they cannot advance professionally in their current business or organization, they might go for work elsewhere, leaving employers to backfill. Employee retention is greatly influenced by a company's ability to offer progression opportunities. A retention plan is not effective if there is no chance for career advancement in the first place.

For experienced professionals, this can be particularly concerning. After many years of service to a company, they likely feel entitled to more than recognition and accolades. They aspire to advance and further their career paths in the same organization. At times, both the employee and employer need to work on leadership training and upskilling. This can be a major roadblock for experienced professionals on their journey to career growth.

The key is to identify where opportunities for professional development exist and seize them when they come. It may require going outside their comfort zones and they must remain open-minded about exploring new directions. Additionally, managers and leaders must stay updated with the latest industry and market trends and understand how their skills can be applied to other areas within the business.

Lack of Exposure to Senior Leadership

Being exposed to senior leadership is essential for managers and leaders to gain insight into the direction of their organization and how decisions are made at higher levels. In addition, they need this information to understand how they can become more aligned with the company's goals.

Senior executives often have more experience and knowledge to help guide managers in their career progression. Additionally, having these valuable connections can open doors for future job opportunities and promotions within the organization or elsewhere. Access to these resources is crucial for people to progress in their careers.

In the organizational hierarchy, managers must consciously network and build relationships with those above them. They must schedule meetings with senior executives and take advantage of opportunities to interact with them. Be proactive in your approach and seek advice from those with more experience than you.

Once these connections are made, it is important to maintain them by staying in touch, sending updates on projects or initiatives you are working on, and requesting feedback whenever possible. It also helps to be open and transparent about your career goals and plans for the future. This will give senior leadership a better understanding of your goals and how they can help you get there.

Lack of Networking Opportunities

No matter how hard you build your resume, if you're not taking advantage of networking opportunities such as industry events or joining a professional organization, it could keep you from getting noticed by recruiters or hiring managers. So, make sure you dedicate time to attend events in your field or join an organization that allows you to build relationships with other professionals in your space. Doing this will allow you to expand your contacts and learn about new job opportunities that may not be advertised.

Additionally, it's important to understand the importance of networking in today's business environment. Your network can provide helpful advice, resources, and knowledge regarding career progression. They can also help connect you with potential employers or customers looking for someone with your skillset and experience. Building relationships is essential if you want to move forward in your career.

Difficulty Finding New Opportunities

Finding new opportunities can be a challenging process, especially for experienced professionals. You may feel overwhelmed when searching for new job openings and need help figuring out where to start. It can also be difficult to determine which skills are most valuable in the current market and how they can help you land your dream job.

Networking is one of the best ways to find new opportunities. This allows you to build relationships with potential employers, colleagues, mentors, and other professionals who could help open doors for you. Additionally, staying active on social media platforms such as LinkedIn or Twitter can expand your reach and let employers know you're an experienced professional looking for new growth opportunities.

Attending industry conferences or seminars is another great way to stay up to date with the latest trends and connect with industry leaders. This can give you a better understanding of the most in-demand skills and how to utilize your experience and knowledge to stand out from other applicants.

By leveraging these strategies, experienced professionals can gain exposure to new opportunities that can help further their careers. You can identify the best options with hard work and dedication while ensuring you maximize your skills, knowledge, and expertise.

Overcoming Imposter Syndrome

Imposter syndrome is an issue many professionals face where they feel inadequate despite having years of experience and expertise under their belt. Unfortunately, this self-doubt often prevents them from seeking new opportunities or taking risks that can lead to career growth.

Experienced professionals must understand the value of their experience and knowledge rather than focusing on what they need to improve in certain areas. There is no perfect job. So, it's important to stay open-minded about the opportunities available and not limit yourself to one particular role or type of work. Additionally, focus on building up your strengths rather than obsessing over weaknesses. Developing confidence in your abilities can help you become more competitive in the job market and give you the courage to take risks that could result in career advancement.

Surround yourself with positive people who support your professional goals and offer constructive feedback when needed. These individuals can become invaluable sources of support and help boost your confidence when times get tough.

By taking these steps to overcome imposter syndrome, experienced professionals can gain the assurance they need to take control of their careers and make the most of their skills, knowledge, and expertise. In addition, they'll be able to pursue new opportunities with a newfound sense of confidence and determination.

Lack of Confidence in Skills and Abilities

Many experienced professionals can feel stuck in their current roles because they need clarification on the strength and relevance of their existing skills and abilities. This lack of confidence can lead to stagnation, making progress difficult.

This can be due to several reasons, such as inadequate job training or needing the right qualifications for current roles. Many managers and leaders may need help demonstrating their expertise after many years on the job. As they become more comfortable with their tasks, they may feel like losing their edge and stagnating in their careers. This can lead to a lack of motivation and prevent them from taking risks or trying new things.

Without any sense of progress, getting and losing sight of what you have already achieved is easy. The key here is to recognize your accomplishments and value your experience while also being open to learning new things. This can help you build your confidence and gain the recognition you deserve. In addition, it is important to keep up with industry trends and news to remain informed of current practices and any changes in your field. Doing this lets you stay ahead of the curve and prepare for new challenges or opportunities.

Perfectionism

Perfectionism is a terrible thing to strive for, which means you always fight to reach the impossible. You'll never be flawless. I am a recovering perfectionist; I realize that. You will never stop being a perfectionist, but you can decrease its effects on your life by being conscious of and consciously managing your unrealistic standards. Perfectionism is a professional and personal prescription for failure, regardless of how you view it.

Being a perfectionist can be both beneficial and detrimental to progressing one's career. On the one hand, it ensures that work is always done to the highest standard; on the other hand, it can make it difficult for individuals to meet deadlines or take risks necessary for their professional growth. Perfectionism can also lead to burnout and frustration when expectations are not met.

Perfectionism can be a major roadblock for experienced professionals looking to expand their careers. Having achieved success in their current role, perfectionists are hesitant to move forward because they fear failing to meet the same high standards they set in the past. As a result, they become risk-averse and strive for perfection rather than progress, which can lead to stagnation in their professional growth.

Lack of Clear Goals

Another common obstacle many experienced professionals face is the need for clear goals. With a plan of action, it can be easy to progress in your career and move forward. However, even if you know what kind of job or role you want to strive towards, it's important to have specific objectives to help guide your actions.

When setting goals, focus on tangible outcomes rather than abstract concepts. For instance, instead of saying, "I want to become better at communication," set an objective such as "I will take a course on effective communication techniques within the next six months."

This allows you to measure the success of your efforts and adjust them accordingly. Additionally, break down large goals into smaller, more achievable tasks. This will keep you motivated and make it easier to track your progress.

Lack of Resources

For many experienced professionals, accessing the necessary resources for furthering their careers can be difficult. Whether it's training materials or industry contacts, these elements are often hard to come by without spending extra money or having certain connections. Sometimes, they may even require relocating to different cities or countries.

Fortunately, the internet has made accessing information much easier and more affordable. A simple Google search can yield a wealth of knowledge on various topics, from fundamentals of management to communication strategies. Additionally, numerous online learning platforms offer courses and resources for professionals looking to improve their skills.

Building your network and connecting with others in your field who can help you is also important. For example, utilize social media sites such as LinkedIn or join professional groups related to your industry to expand your contacts. In some cases, even talking with peers in similar positions can provide valuable insight into how to best manage the challenges associated with progressing one's career.

Lack of Clarity on Job Roles and Responsibilities

Another common challenge experienced professionals face is more clarity on job roles and responsibilities. This often occurs when a company has been around for many years, but no one clearly defines what each person's role should entail.

Sometimes, employees take on additional tasks outside their defined roles to "get ahead" or make themselves more valuable in the organization. Unfortunately, these extra duties can confuse team members and create tension with the management. In addition, it can lead to performance issues if the employee does not have clear direction on how their work should be prioritized or performed.

Your job description sometimes changes as you move up in the organization. This can lead to frustration and feeling disappointed. Therefore, talking to your manager or HR about any job-role discrepancies that may make it difficult for you to progress at work is important.

Experienced professionals must take the initiative and proactively evaluate their responsibilities against their job description to overcome this challenge. They should ensure they understand the expectations of their role and how they fit into the broader organizational objectives. Additionally, they should set realistic goals and create an action plan for meeting them within certain timeframes. Doing so will help keep them on track and allow them to communicate more effectively with management about their performance.

Lack of Support from Management

This can be particularly difficult when you have been with the company for many years and feel your loyalty should be rewarded with development opportunities. Unfortunately, this is only sometimes the case, as managers may be reluctant to invest in training or resources for experienced employees who they think will eventually move on.

The key here is to take control of your career growth by being proactive about learning new skills or information. Invest in yourself by attending seminars, workshops, and conferences related to your field or industry. Additionally, become an advocate for yourself by creating relationships with senior leaders within the organization and sharing successes you have achieved throughout your career path. Doing so will demonstrate your commitment to the organization and your professional development.

02 STRATEGIES TO OVERCOME OBSTACLES

You're in the middle of your professional development, and everything is going according to plan. You're moving at a relaxed speed. Your aims are routinely being met. Your most recent endeavour has finally received approval. Then, you abruptly encounter a hiccup on the road. You can't move ahead any further.

Getting beyond obstacles in your profession is a necessary part of the path. You will inevitably encounter obstacles in your work life, no matter where you are. Some of these may cause you to regress, stop your advancement, or even derail your ambitions. Some obstacles may even cause you to doubt your skills. For example, you can struggle with an overwhelming workload, disagreements with co-workers, or a lack of drive, or you may be trapped in a position that doesn't suit your abilities.

Whatever challenge you're up against at work, it's a necessary step on the road to development and success. There are important lessons to be discovered. And overcoming the challenge can help you advance your abilities. In addition, you'll undoubtedly emerge from it a more improved version of yourself. The following advice can assist you in overcoming any obstacles in your career:

Toss Fear Away

Fear is the first thing that must be conquered to proceed any further. Next, you must have faith in yourself— believing you can overcome challenges.

It's common to feel fear in life. It is what deters people from taking actions that could be harmful. However, you must have the bravery to overcome a challenge in your professional life. It would be best not to let fear stand in the way of formulating rational solutions. Imagine how you will feel once you have overcome the challenge if you are hesitant to face it. Will you feel content? Will you experience relief? Try to concentrate on that sensation and allow it to overpower your fear. Put your head down and face what you're going through if you want to learn from it and move forward.

Expand Your Network with Other Professionals in Your Field

Networking and learning from other professionals are great ways to gain insight into workplace challenges. Others that have experienced similar obstacles can provide valuable advice and support. Broadening your network of acquaintances, especially within the same industry, is an effective method for gathering information about the best strategies for advancing one's career.

Finding out how others overcame similar issues is invaluable insight. Researching online resources such as blogs, podcasts, or online forums dedicated to professional development can help you identify solutions or hear stories of success from people in your sector who have previously encountered the same roadblocks.

View the Obstacle as An Opportunity

A network of nerves in our brain is known as the reticular activating system (RAS). It decides which directions are helpful and which are not after receiving them. This implies that you may train your mind to think positively about challenges. Consider the benefits of taking on the challenge. It can be a chance to pick anything up. It is also a chance for you to showcase your abilities. Having the appropriate mindset is essential to getting beyond obstacles in your job. Even though you may have no control over your environment, you always have control over how you respond.

Create a Plan to Conquer the Challenge

Creating a plan to conquer the challenge can assist you in overcoming it. Take some time to evaluate the situation and come up with realistic solutions. Ensure these are feasible, as setting unrealistic goals may leave you feeling worse off than before. Please make adjustments on your journey as necessary. Utilize resources such as colleagues or mentors who have encountered similar problems in their jobs and try to learn from them. This will help you identify what mistakes to avoid and recognize successes for future challenges. Focus on taking small steps that lead to larger accomplishments over time rather than attempting large feats simultaneously. Record each stage of progress so you can refer back if needed and reflect upon the entire experience.

Don't Take Shortcuts

You might think your present professional setback is leading you to lag. Trying a hasty remedy to get through it can be tempting, but doing so will likely make the issue return. Instead, give the challenge some serious thought. Determine the root reasons, the contributing circumstances, and any viable remedies. When conquering career barriers, it is preferable to move gently and steadily. Shortcuts will only lead to greater difficulties in the long run.

Explore All Possible Routes

Keeping an open mind is one of the keys to overcoming obstacles in your work. You could be accustomed to approaching issues in a certain way, but that approach will work for some problems only sometimes. Exist in any areas where you could make concessions? You can find more viable methods to overcome career problems if you adopt them. Keep trying if your initial attempt at resolving a problem fails. Expand your horizons and try to come up with further solutions. Consider the obstacle from as many perspectives as you can.

Ask Others for Directions

There are some difficulties that are more than what one person can handle. Think about consulting your friends or colleagues for suggestions. They may view the situation from various angles and with varying ideas. Ensure you've thought through the situation before asking for assistance and are not seeking a freebie. Try to repay the favour if they ever ask for assistance in overcoming obstacles in their professional lives.

Keep Your Eyes on the Finish Line

It's simple to lose track of your long-term objectives while dealing with a challenging career. It would be best if you kept the big picture in mind. Remind yourself of your motivations for your actions. Think about the dream you're pursuing for a moment. What actions must you take to make that dream a reality? Your activities should align with your objectives if you want to navigate career obstacles successfully. Staying motivated can help you overcome obstacles, and focusing on your dream can help.

The next time you're in the middle of a career path and encountering a snag, take a moment to breathe. Take each step as it comes, and even though the battle may be protracted, you can be confident that clearing obstacles from your career path is in progress. You can tackle even the most significant challenges with a plan and a clear head.

03 SELF-ASSESSMENT AND REFLECTION

Since success and effectiveness are the foundation of leadership, everyone wants to be a good leader. However, to succeed in a leadership role, a person must first recognize their strengths and shortcomings and work to create common ground. Doing this will vanquish the weakness, and the vulnerable area will strengthen. To succeed, a leader must possess this quality. In leadership, self-reflection and self-assessment are crucial tools with immediate and long-term benefits. This enables a leader to identify areas that require development and the zeal to grow.

Self-reflection and assessment are steps in taking control of your professional growth. It involves evaluating your current strengths and weaknesses, recognizing which areas to work on, and understanding how to use those skills to progress in your career.

Start by inventorying your current skills and competencies, including technical or job-specific skills and interpersonal skills like communication, problem- solving, etc. This will help you create a baseline for yourself to build upon to make improvements.

It would be best to reflect on past successes and failures to identify which strategies worked well for you and which didn't. Finally, consider any feedback from colleagues or supervisors about areas where they think you could improve. This will help you identify any potential roadblocks that may stop you from progressing in your career.

Consider your future goals and how to use current opportunities and resources. Think about the characteristics of different roles or positions that interest you, and plan on how to pursue those areas so that you can continue to grow professionally.

By assessing yourself honestly and critically and planning how to address any challenges or deficiencies, you'll be well on your way to taking control of your professional growth.

PART II

MAKING THE MOST OF YOUR SKILLS, KNOWLEDGE, AND EXPERTISE

04 EXPLORING PROFESSIONAL DEVELOPMENT OPPORTUNITIES

No matter what stage you are in your career, there are always opportunities for professional development. Whether taking advantage of online resources and webinars, attending industry events or networking with peers, staying current on trends and best practices is essential for any manager or leader. Professional development also provides a way to develop new skills and expand your capabilities, helping you to stay current in a rapidly changing workplace. Furthermore, it can help open doors to new opportunities or even catalyze a move up the career ladder.

There are many avenues through which you can explore numerous professional development opportunities. For example, research online or attend local events or workshops to learn more about interesting subjects. You can also ask your colleagues or peers for advice on which courses and seminars may benefit your career growth. Additionally, if you're part of a professional network, there are likely to be many learning opportunities available that you can take advantage of.

No matter what course of action you choose, it's important to remember that professional development is key for any manager or leader looking to progress their career. Investing in yourself and staying current on trends and best practices can help you gain valuable skills and knowledge, ultimately leading to more satisfying career opportunities in the future.

Why is Professional Development Important for Managers and Leaders

Professional development is a key factor in career advancement and growth for managers and leaders. It helps them stay informed and knowledgeable on the latest trends, best practices, and technologies and allows them to expand their skill set. This advanced knowledge can help them to create innovative solutions to problems or meet ambitious goals. Additionally, investing in professional development increases the likelihood of being promoted or offered a higher-level job.

Professional development also helps managers and leaders build their self-confidence, providing them with new skills that may not have been possible in their current roles. By expanding their knowledge base and developing critical thinking skills, they can take on more challenging tasks and lead teams more effectively. Furthermore, learning can help reduce stress levels by giving people an outlet to express themselves and grow professionally.

Professional development allows managers and leaders to network with other professionals in their field. Building relationships with colleagues can provide invaluable insight into trends within the industry and offer advice on navigating career roadblocks. Ultimately, networking can be beneficial during job-seeking or while seeking career opportunities.

Professional development is crucial to any manager or leader's career growth. Investing in yourself and staying current on best practices will pay off in the long run. Professional development gives you the necessary skills and knowledge to succeed and can help you reach your ultimate career goals. Making the most of these opportunities will ensure that you keep progressing along your chosen path.

GOAL SETTING AND TIME MANAGEMENT STRATEGIES

It is often said that setting goals and managing your time are essential components of a successful career. But in the face of many challenges, such as long hours, tight deadlines, or simply too much to do, it can take much work to maintain focus and stay on track.

Goal-setting provides direction and purpose for a career path and helps define success. It also motivates professionals to take ownership of their future while understanding how to contribute to an organization's long-term objectives.

Time management skills are also critical in helping individuals prioritize tasks, manage multiple projects simultaneously, and become more effective in their work responsibilities. Professionals can improve their efficiency and manage their workload by utilizing techniques such as breaking down large tasks into smaller manageable chunks, setting realistic deadlines, and developing a system to track progress.

In addition to goal-setting and time management strategies, experienced managers and leaders must be proactive in taking advantage of the various opportunities presented by their current positions. This could include attending training sessions or workshops; networking with colleagues; participating in mentorship programs; volunteering for additional roles within the organization; or pursuing higher education qualifications that can open up new pathways for career advancement.

By combining strategic planning with effective execution methods, professionals can take control of their future careers and successfully overcome any roadblocks encountered along the way.

The Goal-setting Process

You'll need to set and monitor goals on an ongoing basis. So, why not put up a system for goal-setting that guarantees your team's success?

We set objectives to see an improved or new outcome over a predetermined period. It is a psychological technique to help boost output and performance.

The goal-setting process should begin by identifying the desired outcome, steps, and resources needed. A timeline should also be set for each step to track progress.

Once goals have been established, it's important to remain focused on achieving them. This may require breaking down big tasks into smaller parts or setting up reminders or notifications to stay on track. It is also advisable to review goals occasionally and adjust them if required.

Setting goals encourages people to see them through to completion. Your goals will likely be overlooked if you don't put them down on paper, even if you talk about them with your manager or say something to that effect.

Setting goals at work is crucial for everyone's performance and development and that of the organization as well. Everyone will succeed more if you inspire staff with reasonable and quantifiable goals.

Steps of Goal-setting

Goal setting is a process that involves defining what you want to achieve, developing strategies and plans to reach those goals, and finally, taking action and committing yourself. Here are the steps in detail:

1. Set your goal - This could be a business goal, such as increasing revenue, or an individual goal, like improving customer service skills.
2. Research and plan - Researching the necessary resources, costs, and timelines to reach your target can help create a realistic action plan.
3. Take action - Taking consistent action towards completing milestones within your plan will help keep you motivated and on track to achieving your goal.

4. Monitor progress- Tracking progress against milestones will provide valuable feedback for assessing whether any adjustments are needed to ensure success.

5. Review and adjust - With the feedback received from monitoring, it may be necessary to modify the original plan if things are not going as expected.

6. Celebrate - Remember to celebrate your successes, no matter how big or small your achievement may be. This will boost motivation and help keep morale high throughout the goal-setting process.

Time Management Strategies

Managers have one of the most difficult jobs when balancing their employer's demands and the team's needs. As a result, properly managing your time and team can be a very difficult balancing act. Time management techniques that work can be beneficial.

Knowing what to prioritize in your weekly agenda is a key component of time management. How do you prioritize what needs to be done first regarding strategic planning, contracts, budgets, one-on-one meetings, managing people, staying current with the market, investing time in growing in your role, or attending meetings?

Here are some helpful time management strategies to consider:

1. Focus on the most important tasks - Start with your highest priority and ensure that they get done before moving on to anything else.

2. Create a plan - Create a timeline of tasks and prioritize them according to their importance. This will help ensure you stay focused and organized throughout the day.

3. Set reasonable deadlines - Setting reasonable deadlines can help keep you from feeling overwhelmed, especially if you set yourself up for success by not setting unrealistic goals or deadlines that cannot be met without sacrificing quality.

4. Manage distractions - Identify what distractions may keep you from completing your work and develop strategies for dealing with them effectively. For example, if you are constantly getting interrupted during meetings, consider sending a pre-meeting email to summarize the agenda and then, limit the discussion to what is relevant.

5. Delegate tasks - Be bold and delegate tasks that can be done by someone else. This will free up your time and allow you to focus on more important things.

6. Take breaks - Regular breaks throughout the day will help refresh your mind and energize you to stay productive longer.

7. Be flexible - Some days may not go as planned; unexpected events or changes in priorities may arise, so it's important to remain flexible and adjust your plan accordingly.

Implementing these strategies can help create more balance in your life, allowing you to take control of your career and achieve success.

By focusing on the most important tasks, creating a plan, setting reasonable deadlines, managing distractions, delegating tasks when necessary, taking breaks throughout the day, and remaining flexible when plans change, managers and leaders can work towards their goals while still managing their current responsibilities. With these strategies in mind, they can stay focused and continue confidently progressing in their careers.

BUILDING PROFESSIONAL RELATIONSHIPS AND NETWORKS

When it comes to advancing our careers, building professional relationships and networking are key. Even with 10 or 20 years of experience, we need to create a strong network of contacts who can help us progress in our field. This is why it's so important for us to stay connected and build bridges with like-minded professionals in our industry.

We can start this process by attending conferences, seminars, workshops, and other events related to our field. We can also look for opportunities online, such as joining relevant LinkedIn groups or finding virtual meetups through social media platforms. Building relationships and networks help us learn more about the latest developments in our field, gives us access to mentors, provides support during challenging times, and grants us access to new opportunities and resources.

We can also leverage our existing contacts by asking them for feedback or advice on a project we're working on or seeking their help in finding job opportunities or advancing our careers.

When we reach out to someone with a specific ask, it is more likely that they will be willing to help us out. It's important to remember that networking should not just be about what other people can do for us but also about how we can support others in return.

In addition, if gaps in our experience or skillset stop us from progressing, looking into skill development initiatives such as professional development courses or mentorship programs could be beneficial. Such initiatives can help us acquire new skills and knowledge to help our professional growth.

By building strong relationships and networks and gaining new skills, we can take control of our careers and progress even after years of experience. It's never too late to start!

Tips for Building Strong Relationships

Here are some tips to help you build and maintain relationships that will support your career advancement:

1. **Have a goal in mind**

   Having an end goal before using the tactics below would be best. What do you hope to accomplish by developing relationships? All of these lead to where?

   Are you looking for a new position? Do you want more customers for your company? Is it to look for mentoring? Write out your objectives, whatever they may be. Then, you'll be able to allocate your efforts accordingly and make sure you keep track of your progress in achieving these goals.

2. **Connect on social media**

   Social media is a great way to connect with other professionals in your field – but only if used correctly. Please keep track of industry influencers, the latest news, and trends by following relevant accounts and engaging with them when appropriate. This can help you find people to help you achieve your career objectives.

3. **Network at events and conferences**

   Attending events and conferences related to your profession or industry offers a great opportunity for networking and gaining valuable knowledge from experts in the field. It can also give you access to potential mentors who may be willing to guide and support you on your professional journey.

4. **Keep in touch**

   Once you've made connections, it's important to stay in touch. Please reach out periodically to let them know what you're up to and see how they are doing. This will help strengthen the relationship for further collaboration in the future.

5. **Give back**

   Networking shouldn't only be about taking but also giving back and helping others as much as possible. When you can, offer your skills or knowledge when someone needs help with a project or task related to your field. Doing so builds trust between both parties and creates an atmosphere of mutual exchange that can benefit everyone involved.

   By following these tips and developing strong relationships, you can take control of your career and achieve your professional goal.

PART III

MANAGING YOUR CURRENT JOB

07 NAVIGATING THE WORKPLACE ENVIRONMENT

Managers and leaders who want to progress in their careers must understand their workplace's internal dynamics. This includes understanding how decisions are made, the culture within the organization, and the different personalities that influence daily operations. It also involves awareness of office politics, power plays, and favouritism. Understanding all these elements can help managers effectively navigate their work environment to make informed decisions about their career growth.

Most of us desire a pleasant workplace where we can feel motivated and rewarded for our jobs. However, this frequently doesn't occur at work because of stress, rage, and poor communication. Because of this, managers must foster a positive work environment. Doing this may lower stress levels and foster an atmosphere where everyone feels valued.

Positive Workplace Environment

People who are regarded and valued work in environments conducive to excellent outcomes. Everyone has an equal chance to participate and receive credit for their efforts because responsibilities are clearly defined, expectations are open, and everyone knows what is expected of them.

Mentorship programs that aid staff members in advancing their careers or developing their talents can also be a part of it. A happy work environment promotes productivity and a healthy work-life balance.

Healthy work environments have policies and procedures to deal with employee complaints quickly and successfully. Team activities that emphasize increasing employee involvement foster cooperation among co-workers rather than rivalry. Organizations develop a better working climate where employees enjoy reporting to work each day by laying a strong foundation from the ground up.

Characteristics of a Positive Workplace Environment

The following characteristics are essential for creating a positive workplace environment:

Trust

Trust serves as the cornerstone of a productive work environment. The foundation of positivity is mutual trust, from which the other components flow. In addition, a culture of openness, communication, and respect at all levels characterizes a positive work environment. Employees know their responsibilities and feel free to discuss any questions or concerns with their management. Every employee is willing to operate by the company's principles and standards without hesitation because trust is essential to establishing a great culture.

Cooperation

Cooperation is one of the pillars of a productive workplace. Collaboration fosters initiative, creativity, and teamwork—crucial for professional success. Employees prefer collaboration over competition and work as a team to accomplish shared goals. Employees are encouraged to work as hard as possible in this collaborative setting, which boosts productivity and increases team performance.

Right Behaviour is Encouraged

Positive workplace culture reinforces everyone's good conduct. Employees adhere to the standards and principles of the company. In addition, they must respect everyone, regardless of their rank or status within the organization. Employees working in such an environment are satisfied with putting in long hours and upholding moral standards for themselves and their co-workers. The appropriate behavioural norms, which include accountability and loyalty, are set by the managers and leaders.

Communication

A positive work environment values communication. Building trust, encouraging cooperation and resolving problems all depend on effective communication. Employees can communicate with their bosses and co-workers to cooperate effectively in positive workplace cultures. Task coordination is made possible through open lines of communication, which also boosts employee morale.

Growth

A positive working culture aids the development of the entire team. A healthy work atmosphere encourages original thinking and innovation since everyone strives to increase their knowledge and expertise. Employee development is crucial in a supportive workplace environment since it makes employees feel valued and appreciated. Additionally, it benefits them emotionally and professionally by guaranteeing they are not restricted to consistently finishing the same chores. Additionally, staff may stay current on trends thanks to continuous learning, which boosts productivity and improves outcomes for the company. Finally, any team would benefit greatly from an environment that loves each individual and encourages them to grow.

Everyone Builds Together

The fact that everyone contributes to creating a positive work atmosphere is a key component. The company culture only comes together when everyone actively builds it together, even if managers can explain fundamental values and ensure that employees behave accordingly. Management does not impose a positive company culture on its own. Instead, the team members understand and uphold those beliefs to create a welcoming environment for everybody. It calls for widespread participation from developing the concepts to practicing putting them into action and resolving problems.

Why Should Managers Build a Healthy Workplace Environment?

Managers may create high-value-generating teams by creating a productive workplace with components promoting collaboration. These teams set the bar for creative efficiency while leaving a lasting impression on their bosses.

In addition, building such teams allows managers to realize their full potential for growth since they not only uphold the organization's ideals but also have the gravitas needed to persuade others to join the team and become assets.

More Collaboration and Low Conflicts

As it fosters greater collaboration and less conflict, a positive culture is a great place to work. Since they are certain that supervisors will address their problems appropriately, employees feel safe raising issues. As a result, conflicts and injuries are less likely, which boosts productivity.

Productivity Boost

The productivity of the workforce is increased by creating a healthy workplace culture. They are less susceptible to exhaustion and burnout and avoid existential crises. Employees who work in encouraging and supportive environments tend to be more driven and engaged than those who feel their skills aren't respected at their current jobs. Additionally, they are more inclined to give it their all because they know that doing so will make them happy.

Creative Teams

A healthy workplace environment also supports the development of innovative teams. Employees are receptive to criticism and recommendations, which aids in the creation of creative solutions to issues. This results in improved goods and services that satisfy the requirements of their teams. Additionally, the staff members have confidence in the management and trust them with their ideas.

Low Turnover

A happy workplace also results in low turnover rates, another advantage. Long-term retention rates are higher for employees satisfied with their working conditions. Additionally, they frequently produce more and add value to the team daily. This makes it simpler for managers to maintain efficient operations. Most importantly, a supportive work environment provides value to a team's existence by maintaining it.

Overcome Challenges with Ease

Employees' work environments present substantial challenges to success. A positive culture encourages productivity and lessens the likelihood of conflicts. Employees are less likely to feel frustrated when they know that the management will suitably address their problems.

It encourages effective teamwork and communication, which are crucial for success. When teams are dealing with difficulties, these qualities are essential. A supportive work environment creates the groundwork for values that help teams persevere in facing difficulties.

08 DEVELOPING EFFECTIVE COMMUNICATION SKILLS

Good communication skills are essential for any manager or leader looking for progress in their career. Leaders must convey ideas effectively, collaborate with colleagues, and inspire and motivate those around them. Conversely, poorly developed communication skills can lead to misunderstandings, lack of engagement from team members, decreased trust in the leader's ability, and ultimately, negatively impact performance.

There is a good likelihood that every disagreement, impediment to productivity, error, or misunderstanding in your professional life resulted from miscommunication or might have been avoided with better communication techniques.

Every employee in the office needs to be effective in their communication. Therefore, it would be best to regularly communicate with your staff as a manager to inform them of developments. Your team will feel more confident in an open line of communication if you frequently communicate with them. Additionally, you must be able to represent your team's interests and interact with other managers, teams, and corporate directors.

Benefits of Effective Management Communication

The benefits of strong management communication skills are numerous. Effective communication can help you to:

1. *Improved Team Morale*

Clear communication within a team helps foster better relationships, as members understand each other better and become more comfortable working together. This can lead to increased productivity and morale—key factors in advancing your career.

Without regular manager updates or a forum to voice their problems, a team in the dark without proper communication will lose motivation and become unproductive.

Your team will feel more confident that you are working with them if you have regular one-on-one interactions with them or, at the very least, foster a team culture where you are always accessible for a chat.

2. *A Culture of Effective Communication*

By speaking out, listening intently, and posing pertinent questions, you are sowing the seeds for others to act similarly.

A great strategy to start regular teamwork practices and skills is to run a communication skills course in your company. But like any change in a team's or company's culture, it will take leadership commitment to keep the change going.

You must continue to make effective communication a priority and set expectations for your team members. It is also a great way to allow them to practice their communication skills while developing better relationships.

3. *Clear Purpose and Direction*

Your frequent updates will direct the team's course of action. Your communication will ensure the team knows exactly what is expected of them. As a result, there will be more movement and less confusion when everyone is on the same page.

Also, by keeping your team updated on performance metrics and providing resources to help them, you can ensure they meet their goals promptly. The clearer the expectations are, the less likely they will be derailed by false starts or lack of direction.

4.   *Higher levels of productivity*

Greater productivity results from more deliberate action. Clear communication and an active listening culture will streamline operations and improve accuracy across the board.

No one enjoys working on a task with no clue as to why it is important or how it fits into the overall vision for the project. By providing context and communication about objectives, you can help your team work smarter and faster toward the end goal.

5.   *Early resolution of problems*

No manager enjoys dealing with discord on their team. But, unfortunately, it is inevitable even in the most harmonious of teams.

The issue can be remedied with the least disturbance if you can spot possible conflict areas or poor performance early on and manage these challenging conversations easily and professionally.

Regular, effective communication with your team can also help you to anticipate potential issues and develop strategies to avoid them. This proactive approach will ensure the team runs smoothly and prevent problems from escalating into bigger issues.

6.   *Sustainable savings*

Looking at the above advantages, you'll notice that each advantage contributes to less time and money wasted, happier employees, and a productivity-oriented mindset.

With an enduring and satisfying culture, your team will save time and money and benefit your company.

This is an invaluable skill to have as a leader, and it will help you move up the corporate ladder and improve your team's performance and morale in the long run.

A more efficient and productive team can mean higher profits for your company, making it well worth the time spent improving communication practices.

7. Improved reputation

The benefits of fostering better communication among your team extend far beyond financial gains. When teams communicate effectively and manage their workloads efficiently, they become highly regarded by their colleagues – both within and outside.

A strong reputation among colleagues provides tangible results like greater opportunities for career advancement or being considered for leadership roles. This a great way to demonstrate your team's excellent communication and valuable reputation.

In conclusion, effective communication is one of the most important elements of successful management and leadership. With the right attitude, knowledge, and strategies, you can ensure everyone on your team works together more cohesively while improving productivity and gaining a better reputation among colleagues.

Essential Skills for Communication

Here are items you'll need in your toolbox if you wish to adopt the "communication superhero" style of management:

An Understanding of Different Styles

Everybody communicates uniquely. Learn about the various communication nuances to recognize your communication style and the styles of the people you supervise.

Understanding and improving communication between you and those you lead begins with this skill.

Understanding different communication styles are key to developing relationships and creating effective teams. For example, some people may be more direct and to the point. In contrast, others take a more subtle approach to getting the point across; understanding the difference between these two helps in better communication.

Moreover, listening is just as important as speaking regarding effective communication. Listening carefully goes beyond simply hearing what someone has to say; it also involves paying attention to body language, tone of voice, and facial expression. This allows one to understand the underlying messages being conveyed and respond accordingly.

Ability to Identify and Overcome Barriers

Poor communication obstacles can significantly reduce your company's production.

Barriers might include one person needing to pay more attention during a conversation, overusing jargon and buzzwords, to needing help comprehending another's point of view. As a manager, you must be able to successfully negotiate these obstacles anytime they present themselves to ensure productivity.

To overcome communication obstacles, you must acknowledge and proactively address them. This can include active listening (ensuring everyone is heard) and clarifying points of view by asking questions, summarizing what was said, or repeating key points. It would be best to encourage others to do the same. By modelling this behaviour; you can help create a more respectful environment where people feel comfortable expressing their ideas without fear of judgment or ridicule.

Clarity in Your Communications

Clear communication is the cornerstone of effective communication. We all want to speak clearly. Yet, it can be difficult to master and maintain effective communication in the workplace. To improve your clarity, practice speaking slowly and articulating your thoughts. Check for understanding when asking questions or making statements: "Does that make sense?" "Are we all on the same page?"

Additionally, be aware of potential communication pitfalls such as using confusing language or repeating yourself too often. If you find yourself in a complex conversation, simplify it by breaking it into manageable chunks with key points highlighted.

When possible, use visual aids to help explain concepts more clearly. Also, remember that effective communication goes both ways; ask questions if you need help understanding something and remain open-minded when someone else does the same.

Accurate Questioning Skills

A task or problem can sometimes be understood by asking the correct questions.

Everyone can save time, angst, and wasted effort if they know how to ask intelligent questions that yield the information you need to move a work or issue forward.

When asking questions, start with open-ended questions that allow the other person to explain their thoughts more freely. Ask for clarification if something isn't clear, and avoid making assumptions.

Questions should also be specific and focused on one topic at a time to maintain focus and save precious time.

Active Listening Abilities

How much of what you consider listening are you waiting for your moment to speak? Do you ever mentally list your upcoming tasks as someone speaks to you?

If the answer is yes, you're not alone!

For the majority of us, active listening is undoubtedly an acquired talent. It can increase productivity and make everyone's day simpler, much like precise questioning, summarizing, and note-taking during conversations.

To become a better listener, start by paying attention to the speaker's words without judgment or bias. Focus solely on the other person rather than formulating an answer or calculating what you will say next. It also helps if you repeat what the speaker said before giving your opinion; this will ensure that both of you are on the same page and help prevent misunderstandings.

Moreover, apply 'active' listening techniques such as asking relevant questions and making meaningful statements about what was said before offering your opinion or feedback. Showing genuine interest in their ideas and perspective will help build trust between you and the other person, which can prove invaluable regarding career growth and advancement.

Ultimately, being an active listener will show that you care about the speaker's thoughts and opinions, which can help build strong relationships with colleagues, bosses, and customers. Additionally, mastering this skill will allow you to make better decisions in your professional life and identify potential opportunities for growth or development. So, hone your listening skills to get ahead in your career!

Rapport-building Techniques

Developing solid working connections with your team members and team building go hand in hand. You'll build a good, constructive rapport with each team member through regular communication and showing that you care about their opinion.

To do this effectively, start by respecting everyone's skills, knowledge, and opinions. Respect the ideas of others, even if they are different from your own, and be willing to explore other perspectives before making a decision.

Furthermore, have an open mind when it comes to new ideas. Try not to get stuck in old routines or comfortable habits. Instead, embrace change as a chance for growth and improvement. Finally, practice gratitude—express appreciation for your team members who contribute positively towards the company's goals. This will help foster positive energy and collaboration!

All these will help build relationships you and your team can rely on and trust. A strong rapport built across the team makes communication easier and everyone's ideas respected. This facilitates faster decision-making processes, which is vital to career development and progression.

MAKING THE MOST OF YOUR ROLE AND CAREER PATH

Being in a job for many years can have both benefits and drawbacks. On the one hand, you'll have built up considerable experience and knowledge, which is invaluable when it comes to getting ahead. But on the other hand, being comfortable in your role can make it difficult to break out of entrenched habits or push yourself beyond your comfort zone.

The challenge for experienced professionals is ensuring that their skills and knowledge remain relevant and that they keep progressing in their careers.

Managers are experts who inspire, guide and control a team of experts. You might improve your team's performance by developing your managerial skills. In this post, we'll discuss why it's critical to develop as a manager, go over advice for new managers, outline what it takes to be an effective manager and outline a process.

Why is It Important to Improve as a Manager?

As a manager, you should develop because your duties could shift over time. New team members and new personalities may help your team grow. Increasing your capacity for job tasks, becoming a supervisor whom people enjoy working for, and learning to adapt to new scenarios are all aspects of becoming a better manager. First-time managers must remember that there are still greater career ambitions you can seek through professional development and progress.

How to Be An Effective Manager?

Whether you're brand-new to the position or have been managing for some time, here are some tips to help you be the most effective manager you can be:

1. Get to know everyone and adapt to their work styles

It's a good idea to spend the first day of your new job getting to know your team and learning about their responsibilities. Most, if not all, of the people you're responsible for managing, may already be familiar to you, but you need to learn their working habits. To make the transition smoother, figure out how to match your working style with your staff. Then, in order for your staff to identify adjustments for themselves or for you to make, you must explain your strategy to them in a way that considers their employment.

2. Delegate effectively

Your duties as a manager could be centred on achieving broad goals. A great manager includes breaking down big goals into manageable, smaller steps. It's your best advantage to delegate constructively since someone on your team can complete the task incredibly well. Think about watching your team members first to see who is best at what.

3. Talk to other managers in a similar role

You can gain insight into what is proper and what is expected in your new role by speaking with managers at the same level.

Meeting with them immediately is a good idea because they could provide advice for your initial few weeks. After that, consider contacting them frequently to get their opinions and thoughts and ask management questions.

4. Balance independence and oversight with your employees

It is crucial to respect your employees' autonomy while also assuming how much direction they'll require. Finding the optimal strategy to meet different employee preferences, such as more or less oversight, may take some time. Strive to know who functions best when left alone and who gains from regular meetings with you.

5.   Involve employees in identifying departmental strengths and weaknesses

It's critical for a new manager to understand all of the department's strengths and shortcomings. Because they are familiar with the department and will be impacted by any changes, consider incorporating your staff. Consider allowing time for everyone to speak during your first meeting. They can talk about improvements they want to see or items they want to retain.

6.   Establish clear channels of communication

Talk about your preferred means of contact, such as email. Your team colleagues will be able to reach you easily as a result.

If you have the time, you can create a rule stating that anyone is welcome to come into your office and speak with you, but you might find it easier to mandate that staff members attempt to reply to all emails within an hour of receiving them.

7.   Be accountable

Accepting accountability for your deeds is crucial early on in your new position. For example, if you're having trouble in your new position or made a mistake, own it and explain how you intend to fix it. This can demonstrate to your team that you are reliable and trustworthy.

8.   Give constructive feedback frequently

When employees receive constructive feedback frequently, you may anticipate their skill development will occur more quickly. A performance review is often a comprehensive evaluation your firm might employ on a certain occasion, like an annual review.

Based on your observations, you might develop your approach to providing feedback more frequently. For instance, establish team objectives and hold regular check-ins when discussing each member's progress.

9.   Adjust your work relationships accordingly

You should modify your interpersonal skills after being promoted to manager. For instance, your communication style and frequency may alter if you worked on a team which you now lead. Preparation for this adjustment beforehand could be useful if you want to feel ready.

10.   Lead by example

Set a good example as a manager for your staff to follow. For instance, if you instruct your group to use an email signature, remember to include one of your own. In addition, you can aid in their reinforcement by modelling the patterns you want to see.

11.   Stay in contact with your former supervisor

Maintaining communication with your former boss can make it easier for you to transition to your new position. This is because they can give guidance based on their management experience as well as their management of you. In particular, if you both work for the same business, they advise you on particular managing jobs.

12.   Remind employees of the company's objectives and goals

You can see the organization's goals more broadly in your manager's capacity. You can remind your staff to apply such ideas to their work. You may explain the company's objectives and how they relate to them. Based on the overall corporate objectives, you can also develop team goals.

13. Listen to your employees' career goals

As a manager, some responsibilities provide you with the opportunity to act as a mentor, which includes taking an interest in the career goals of your staff. This is something to bear in mind while appointing new tasks. For instance, giving them responsibilities connected to their areas of strength can motivate them to grow in those areas. I suggest that they get promotions to help them advance in their careers.

14. Encourage teamwork

The performance of your staff can be improved through teamwork, enabling them to work well with other departments. More effective team collaboration can hasten approvals and design workflows that are more effective.

Consider employing team-building exercises or facilitating training sessions to improve your staff's collaboration abilities.

15. Resolve conflicts effectively

It's crucial to acknowledge the presence of conflict in the workplace. Your organization may have policies in place for certain circumstances. Depending on the circumstance, ask an HR specialist or an independent mediator to resolve this kind of conflict.

As a manager, you can assist in settling minor disputes on your team or design training courses to aid in developing your team members' conflict-resolution abilities.

16. Stay in contact with your direct supervisor

Remember that your supervisor supports you, and you are not making decisions alone. One of your duties is to report the progress of your team. Meeting your boss to discuss goals and priorities is also a smart idea. Doing this lets you stay informed and increases your confidence when making adjustments.

17.   *Separate your priorities from that of your employees*

Since managers' duties frequently have shifting priority levels, time management is an important skill. Before stepping in to help an employee having trouble, attempt to encourage them to find a solution. While assisting your colleagues in need is undoubtedly your priority, strive to focus on your more pressing obligations.

18.   *Let your employees know the impact of their work*

Thanks to your managerial perspective, you can put your team's work in a broader context. Making employees feel like they are a part of the bigger team that makes up the firm is a terrific motivating approach. You can explain how their efforts impact other business areas and how your team supports the latter's objectives.

STRATEGIC CAREER PLANNING

10 CREATING A VISION AND PLAN TO PROGRESS YOUR CAREER

You may advance in your job by setting clear, quantifiable goals. Even though creating a career plan can take much work, it will pay off by enabling you to comprehend where you desire your profession to go and what you need to accomplish to get there.

Even if you haven't yet discovered your dream job, you can feel inspired by developing and implementing an employee career development plan because it will help you create specific strategies.

You can utilize a career development plan to construct a roadmap for your professional life. Typical professional development plan examples include the following:

- **The Starting Point:** Where do you presently stand in your professional journey, considering the past experiences and skills that have shaped your career?
- **The Destination:** Where do you want to go in your career, and which skills and experience do you need to get there?
- **The Gap:** The obstacles you must overcome to reach the destination, such as a lack of skills, experience, or credentials.
- **The Route:** How to close the gap to reach your intended destination—the steps you must take to fill the voids in your qualifications and skills, such as taking a course or obtaining certifications.
- **The Timeline:** How much time do you want to commit to developing yourself professionally, and when will you reach your goals?

Create your individualized roadmap to success with a personalized development plan. It will aid you in recognizing attainable career aspirations and crafting and executing the plans to get there!

How to Create a Career Development Plan?

To develop an effective career plan, adhere to the following instructions:

1. *Identify your current position*

The initial step in any professional development plan is recognizing your current status. With this action, you can assess and appreciate your strengths and abilities. It will also help you comprehend the areas that need improvement and identify potential paths. You can use tools such as your employee review, a job analysis tool, or self-assessments to gain insight into where you stand professionally.

At this stage, you should consider questions like:

- What skills do I need to develop?
- What experience do I currently have?
- How can I translate my skills and experience into something new or different?
- What are the most important areas I should focus my attention on?

Invest a few minutes in jotting down the answers to these queries. Then, compose your current standing in your profession, including if you have concluded any schooling or are interested in pursuing further graduate schooling and where exactly you stand on the career ladder.

2. *Identify your destination*

When creating a career development plan, the next step should be determining where you want to go. Defining your destination is vital in recognizing and taking advantage of beneficial opportunities that can help you reach it.

Carefully reflect on what kind of job or role you would like to have. Then, consider the skills and qualifications needed for this role and the ways you can acquire these skills.

Determine your career goals by carrying out the following actions:

Brainstorm

Get rid of any barriers or restraints that may be keeping you back. What is your ideal line of work? Where would you like to be in five to ten years if nothing prevented it? List your long-term professional objective. If becoming the CEO of a midsize company is your dream or if you want to become a master of another language, include these things in your strategy. Develop more specific goals in the form of concise statements.

Establishing your desired location in minor steps can be useful. For example, where do you want your career to be in two years, given where you are now and your current skill set? Visualizing is simpler because this increase is sufficiently close to your daily life.

Consider the next five to ten years

Consider where you want to be in five to ten years from now. This bigger step will require you to consider potential opportunities that might present themselves two or three steps down the road. For example, would you prefer to continue working for your current firm but in a more senior capacity? Do you desire employment with a different business? Or you may want to change careers completely. Again, ensure your stated objectives are consistent with the things that are most inspiring to you.

Understanding your skills and the job alternatives available once you have finished the first two steps would be better. In addition, you can now consider the best way to get to your desired location.

3.   *Do a gap analysis*

A gap analysis is a form of objective assessment that helps recognize the difference between where you are and where you want to be. It will help determine the skills you need to develop or gain to succeed in your desired career.

You are now prepared to do a gap analysis, establishing where you are and where you want to be. To finish a gap analysis, take the following actions:

Research Your Career Goal

Find job ads for the position you want, keeping in mind your two- or five-year career focus goals. Ensure that the requirements align with your end goal and that the descriptions correspond to your abilities and expertise.

Consult with Seasoned Professionals

Spend some time talking to your mentor, boss, and co-workers to determine if there are any important things you should add to the list. For example, even if you might not want to inform your boss that you want to move on to a position with a higher salary at another organization, you can still discuss with them the particular abilities you would like to bring to your current position.

Your supervisor will probably be happy to assist you in finding resources or give you pertinent responsibilities because this type of professional development would benefit your team, the firm, and you individually.

Rate Your Qualifications

Once you've compiled this list of qualifications, go over it line by line and compare your present knowledge, training, and experience to the demands. Make a basic rating scale of 1 to 5, with 1 denoting a complete mismatch between you and the demand and 5 denoting a great match. With this approach, you will need to put more time and effort into improving the lower rating aspects about you.

Identify Gaps and Determine Patterns

Once you've finished this activity, list the areas where you need to grow. Find individuals who have similar experiences and skills and group them. You'll start to see trends in which knowledge or experiences you already have a strong foundation and which ones need more work.

Check to see whether anything needs to happen in a specific order. For instance, you'll need to learn how to utilize a certain software before taking on additional duties at work connected to it. You must concentrate on the following list of abilities, credentials, and work experience.

4.   *Create your career development plan*

You are prepared to create a plan to progress in your profession now that you know the specific abilities you must acquire. Create a clear plan to achieve your career goals using the list of abilities, knowledge, and experiences you hope to acquire over the coming years in this stage. What you should do is:

Set Small Task-oriented Goals

Develop a series of tasks for each item on the list to enable you to do it. For instance, if one of the talents you'd like to develop is using a certain piece of software, your plan might entail enrolling in a course to learn about it, practising with a colleague, and asking your manager for permission to use the program as part of your job.

Organize with a Timeline

By the logical trajectory for your goals, arrange the strategy like a timeline. For example, start with short-term goals you can accomplish fairly quickly, like reading a book, and work your way up to longer-term objectives, like earning a master's degree.

Think Smart

You can develop attainable goals with the help of the SMART goal template. Smart, Measurable, Achievable, Relevant, and Time-bound are the acronym for SMART goals. For example, a SMART goal is to work one-on-one with your boss to better your understanding of the payroll system at your organization. Using the SMART goal-setting form, you can ensure that your objectives are measurable and doable within a given time.

Create Task Deadlines

Setting deadlines for each work is the greatest way to ensure you stick to the plan. Set a deadline for when you should begin working on a task. Plan out any prerequisites for each item as well. For instance, you might need to fill out an application and buy the necessary materials before you sign up for a professional development course. You currently have a plan for your professional development.

5. Measure your progress and be ready to re-evaluate

Checking your progress is critical to keeping your career development plan on track. Compare the tasks you've achieved to those that remain and note any significant milestones. It would be best if you were ready for changes as well. Your professional goals might change because of shifting trends or unexpected opportunities. If this happens, don't hesitate to re-evaluate and update your timeline.

Although you will undoubtedly encounter obstacles as you build your career, don't be overwhelmed; use this guide to set a course for success. Each time you complete a task on your plan, it should bring you closer to attaining your desired professional success.

Once you've designed your career growth plan, it doesn't end there. The following actions now signal the start of the implementation stage:

Keep Track

Remember how your implementation compares to the deadlines you gave yourself in step four to hold yourself accountable. Then, to ensure you continue to meet the deadline, check in with the list at least twice a year.

Consider Milestones

Once you've started reviewing your list of abilities, credentials, and work experience, you'll want to figure out how to gauge your professional development. Metrics for work success include earning a good performance evaluation, getting hired, getting promoted, making connections that will help you in your career, or winning an award.

Update Goals Accordingly

There will be unforeseen occurrences and events. For example, a job opportunity can unexpectedly divert your career, or you might have to relocate. Many different things could cause your plan to fail. Remember that you can change course as long as you continue to adapt. The plan is not set in stone. Therefore, revisiting it to adjust your objectives to reflect your current situation is a good idea. Plan to review the plan itself around every six months and make any necessary adjustments to suit your current goals, and track your progress regularly.

11 LEVERAGING YOUR STRENGTHS, SKILLS, AND EXPERTISE

Whatever be your career level or experience, leveraging your existing skills, knowledge, and expertise is important. Taking stock of your accomplishments can help identify areas where you excel, making it easier to target opportunities that best fit your strengths.

Employers require workers with a variety of skill sets to improve their businesses. Both you and your employer benefit from your abilities in the workplace. You can set professional goals and identify the appropriate job to exploit your abilities in the workplace once you learn to use those skills to your advantage.

Being honest and taking stock of your skills can also help you understand what career paths make the most sense. It would be best to capitalize on professional strengths instead of developing new skills or knowledge, which may take time. Leveraging existing knowledge helps build confidence and momentum, which could lead to more success down the line.

Sometimes, a lack of confidence or uncertainty can cause professionals to hesitate when presented with career opportunities. To move forward with greater assurance, one must be aware of one's abilities and expertise and not underestimate them. This will enable managers and leaders to take calculated risks when advancing their career paths.

The Importance of Leveraging Your Strengths in the Workplace

Using your advantages in the workplace will help you succeed in your position. Knowing your strongest skills will help you accomplish everyday activities more effectively, create goals for professional advancement within your current organization or in a different one, and improve your job satisfaction.

You benefit from using your strengths in the job in the following ways:

Helps You Find the Best Role

You're more likely to discover a career that perfectly fits your abilities and interests if you use your strengths to your advantage when looking for work. So go after positions that substantially rely on your best skills.

Increases Your Productivity

If you set goals to concentrate on your strongest skills to complete daily chores, working in a position that matches your strengths makes you more productive.

Sets You Up for Leadership

Leaders are adept at utilizing both their own and others' abilities. To recognize and develop their team's capabilities, they serve as mentors.

Allows You to Grow

You can progress toward realizing your potential at work by utilizing your strengths to maximize your work experience.

How to Leverage Your Strengths

Everyone has unique talents hidden inside them, and honing these abilities can give you a tremendous advantage in the workplace. Here's how to leverage your strengths for success:

1.   Define your strengths

If you wish to benefit from your talents, it is essential that you first comprehend your distinct capabilities.

There are many ways including self-assessment, performance reviews, and feedback from colleagues and mentors to uncover what makes you special and take advantage of those strengths.

2.   Set professional goals

A manager can assist you in creating goals that play to your abilities. Then, with the help of your manager, talk about these strengths and concentrate on developing work tactics that will help you advance professionally. Spend time on these objectives year-round rather than just during annual reviews. Seek feedback as you continue to play to your strengths to accomplish your career goals. Building on your skills is critical regardless of your position within the organization.

3.   Show evidence of your strengths

Decide which of your strengths you use most frequently at work now. Next, discover the attitudes and actions that enable you to use these abilities. Then, decide what proof you can present to support your professional qualities. Finally, when you recognize your strengths' good effects on your work, plan to produce more fruitful results.

4.   Strengthen your strengths

Find ways to grow what you are already good at by working to improve it. For example, take part in advanced training to develop your strongest skills. You might even offer to teach or mentor others in your specialized areas. Your knowledge immediately grows when you can use your strengths to teach someone else.

5.   *Choose strength-building behaviours*

Your actions and routines may alter how you use your advantages. For instance, if you read books and articles written by professionals in your sector, you can hone certain abilities you want to develop. Concentrate on positive work habits that facilitate your ability to utilize your abilities.

12   TAKING CONTROL OF YOUR PROFESSIONAL GROWTH

You would have unlimited control over your professional life in a perfect world. But occasionally, life happens, and your career takes a surprising turn. It can be incredibly frustrating to experience a roadblock in your career development, especially after years of hard work and dedication.

Before you start feeling discouraged, it's important to remember that most professionals will face at least one roadblock during their career journey. Understanding how to identify these common challenges, develop strategies to overcome them, and take control of your professional growth is key to long-term success.

If you want to take charge of your career, being proactive can significantly impact how it develops.

These are five suggestions for managing your career:

1. *Make a concrete plan*

You can plan for the future you want by creating a career plan that includes both your short- and long-term goals.

Undoubtedly, it's nice to daydream about your ideal profession, but you can take control of your career by developing a clear plan that defines exactly what you need to accomplish and when you need to do it. In addition, an actionable plan outlining your short- and long-term goals can help you stay on track and determine how to move forward when roadblocks happen.

2. *Assess your strengths and goals*

List your advantages and disadvantages. Afterwards, incorporate goals that will aid you in overcoming the weaknesses in your career plan. For example, do you require greater expertise in a certain field? Could you please fill that gap? Would obtaining a new certification let you take charge of your professional future? Look for courses that can aid in your knowledge acquisition.

Furthermore, if you have everything, you must take charge of your job; great! You can use that knowledge to guide you down your desired professional path.

3. *Practice patience*

Anything worth achieving most often takes some time. In the same way, give your career plan time to take root and blossom after you've developed a strategy and decided how to move forward.

Even though the waiting game can be challenging, things rarely proceed as rapidly as you would like. So, don't let impatience get the best of you. Instead, maintain your focus and monitor your progress to stay on track with your objectives.

4. *Change at Any Age*

Switching careers is always possible if you need a different path.

If life allows you to restart your career, take it! With the current technological leaps and the widespread use of remote working methods, now is a great time to reinvent yourself. Take some time to research and investigate different paths that might be suited for your skillset, and don't be afraid to make changes when necessary.

5. *Embrace Your Fears*

Although it may seem absurd, fear can be a strong motivator to keep you moving toward your goals. So, don't avoid aspects of your job search that could make you uncomfortable as you attempt to take control of your career, especially if you're moving forward with a new line of employment.

The easiest strategy to avoid burnout at work is to take charge of your career path. You can maintain control and achieve success by defining your goals and developing a clear plan.

PART V

MODERN-DAY WORKPLACE

13 REMOTE WORKING

The pandemic changed how we perceive work, making distinguishing between the actual workplace and the physical office harder. As a result, the line between personal and professional life became blurred.

Companies started introducing a new digital workplace environment as people connect and collaborate in previously unheard-of ways.

The traditional in-office setting will eventually give way to a digital workplace. It includes all tasks that individuals perform in an actual office, but they do them electronically using digital workplace solutions.

Examples of straightforward digital workplace solutions are project management software, e-learning platforms, and online collaboration tools. If properly applied, these solutions can aid firms in boosting their productivity, revenue, agility, and flexibility—and even help them scale their operations.

What Does It Mean to Work Remotely?

A professional setting known as "remote work" allows employees to do their business from their homes or any other place other than the actual office of their employer. It frequently entails setting up a workspace at home. Nevertheless, working remotely doesn't have to be restricted to your home.

Remote work is a common alternative for "digital nomads," who work from wherever they are and move often. For example, they might operate from hotels, beach clubs, coffee shops, or airport lounges instead of a home office.

This type of remote labour would have been difficult in the past due to resource and technological limitations. However, more employees can now work remotely and collaborate on the go thanks to collaboration apps like Slack and Zoom that have helped close the technology gap.

In the remote workplace, managers should emphasize employee communication and engagement. Managers must also focus on tracking productivity, setting deadlines, and holding employees accountable for their work output. These tactics can help build a successful remote working environment when done correctly.

Managers must create an atmosphere that encourages people to communicate with each other and be open about their progress on projects. Furthermore, they must ensure that team members get along well with one another since tensions within the group can cause difficulties. Additionally, there must be regular check-ins and feedback sessions or assessments for team members to stay connected and productive.

Understanding how different types of workers engage remotely is vital since everyone has different ways of working. For example, some prefer to work alone, while others feel more productive in a team environment. Therefore, managers need to understand the needs and preferences of their teams so that they can create an effective remote working environment.

14 UPSKILLING

Employees' talents are expanded, and skill gaps are reduced through training programs and professional development opportunities offered as part of the upskilling trend, promoting continual workplace learning. Upskilling concentrates on enhancing the skill sets of present employees, typically through training, so that they can progress in their professions and discover new roles and possibilities within the organization.

Businesses must fill these new positions with applicants who have the pertinent, specialized skill sets as technology offers new opportunities and career positions within the workplace. By upskilling their staff, businesses may preserve their present workforce, create possibilities for employee growth, and fill these unfilled roles while bridging the digital talent gap.

Professionals must make the most of their upskilling opportunities, especially if they are unfamiliar with the technology. Courses on the latest software and programs can give them a competitive edge in the job market and allow them to progress in their careers. Additionally, staying abreast of industry trends and developments will enable professionals to place themselves ahead of the curve when considering career advancement. Finally, understanding new technologies helps professionals present themselves as knowledgeable problem-solvers with good decision-making skills – invaluable for achieving career success.

Why is Upskilling Important?

Technology is still fast altering how most firms function. As a result, businesses and their staff members must constantly expand their technical know-how and skill sets. Eventually, companies are compelled to either locate new talent or upgrade existing employees' skills to bridge the skills gap when the job needs to evolve and new ones become necessary.

By improving the skills of its present employees through upskilling, businesses can save money by avoiding the time and expense of acquiring new personnel. The present workforce has higher expectations for employment than a steady paycheck and a pleasant working environment. Today's workers look forward to benefits like paid holidays, accessible healthcare, and professional development. Organizations can help workers feel appreciated and feel like they have a bright future in the firm by giving them opportunities for upskill training, which can lead to internal promotions and raises.

Upskilling also offers members of the staff the chance to remain current in an ever-evolving business environment. Keeping up with new technology and trends may help professionals stay competitive and relevant, making them more attractive candidates when they look for other job roles.

Developing An Upskilling Strategy

Companies must first determine the existing skill gaps within their business before implementing an upskilling strategy. By taking this step, firms can ensure that their efforts to upskill their personnel align with those needs.

Next, businesses must consider the upskilling initiatives' immediate and long-term effects. For instance, it can be simple to concentrate on the newest tool available, but this advancement might only benefit the company in the short run. To increase long-term value, a business should concentrate on how to improve its core competencies. To keep a competitive edge for the business, utilizing new technology and staying current with industry trends is vital.

Once the skill gaps have been identified, a firm can start developing and choosing the training programs that make the most sense for the organization. The secret is to organize training and development to benefit the business.

15 ONLINE CERTIFICATION

Online certifications can help experienced professionals break out of a career rut and strengthen their skills. They provide in-depth training on topics related to the individual's field, such as project management, customer service, or marketing. Such courses allow professionals to stay up-to-date with developments in their area and use this knowledge to add value to their current roles. In addition, these courses help build confidence and demonstrate an individual's commitment to professional development.

Have you considered devoting time to getting a professional certification?

It's good to know that you have thought about this. You are on the correct path. You can enrol in a course in your chosen subject area or broaden your horizons by learning a new skill.

Obtaining a new certification or specialized expertise has many benefits and only some downsides. You will only benefit if you put your time, money, effort, and enthusiasm into obtaining professional credentials. But, on the other hand, you will always take advantage of opportunities, too.

Certification has many advantages, and we list our top five advantages below.

1.   *Learn new skills*

One of the most obvious advantages of certificates is this. Human life depends on learning new abilities, which implies you are constantly expanding your knowledge.

Your self-esteem can significantly increase by picking up new talents and getting certifications. In addition to the value you get from your skills, you also get validation.

Because certification places a strong emphasis on lifelong learning, it is crucial.

You can increase your job capabilities and responsibilities by learning new skills. In addition to what you are accustomed to doing, you will be equipped and prepared to handle other elements of your organization.

For instance, there are countless advantages to corporate training. Improvements in sales, management, finance, human resources, and many other crucial business abilities can be among them.

Whatever new talents you decide to master, sign up for a certification course to demonstrate your in-depth familiarity with the subject.

2. *Improve your resume*

It takes time to adequately describe the positive impact a new certification can have on your resume.

Obtaining enough additional qualifications may alter the format and appearance of your CV. Therefore, you can add a specific area to your resume where you can detail your qualifications and certifications.

In the job, having documentation proving you know the ins and outs of a particular talent is crucial. One of the numerous advantages of certificates is the opportunity to enhance your resume significantly.

In addition to your schooling and work experience, including a professional certification on your CV will give the impression that you are a very capable employee.

When a candidate demonstrates their qualifications, employers hire them right away. But they are even more eager to hire someone who demonstrates their qualifications and dedication to continuing their education.

Attending voluntary professional certification courses demonstrates your commitment to lifelong growth.

Your resume will always be fresh and active. But instead, you'll constantly seek opportunities to expand your knowledge and skill set.

3.   *Command authority*

One of the finest methods to move up the ladder is to increase your status by learning more.

Increased status level brought on by having more courses under your belt is one of the greatest advantages of certifications.

The ability to add a certification to your name or resume commands authority and demonstrates your credibility to potential clients. People will respect and trust you to do the task if you have established trust with them.

One of the additional advantages of certificates is this. Even though you might not decide to pursue a professional certification just for this purpose, it is undoubtedly a great side benefit.

When you demonstrate that you have credentials to support your abilities, it establishes your authority and establishes you as a force to be taken seriously.

4.   *Boost productivity*

It's easy. You'll be more effective at what you do if you know what you're doing. You can complete a task more swiftly and effectively when you are well-trained.

One further advantage of certificates is an increase in production.

You may not have signed up for a certification course specifically for this benefit, but you will undoubtedly get it in addition to the sense of achievement.

Your life and job will improve if you work more productively and efficiently. For instance, if a worker has a certain software or program certification, they can not only complete routine jobs more rapidly, but also benefit from the program's more sophisticated features.

Using programs to their maximum potential results in better work completed in less time. And that is something that every successful business should aim to achieve!

5. *Have an edge over the competition*

The edge you gain over your competition is another one of the enormous advantages of certifications. Who are employers ultimately looking to hire? And from which companies do consumers want to make purchases?

Everybody wants to conduct business with the most capable and reliable choice. If you have professional certifications to support your knowledge, you are already lightyears ahead of those who do not.

Also, starting early can provide you with an advantage over your competitors. For example, high school students are increasingly pursuing certifications so that, when they graduate, they will be distinguished from their peers by having particular skills to their name.

Benefits of Online Certifications for Experienced Professionals

For experienced professionals, online certifications can offer several benefits. For instance, it allows them to stay current on their field's latest trends and technologies. In addition, online certifications allow them to exercise and strengthen their skills without taking time away from work or family life.

1. *Refresh your knowledge*

Many industries constantly change and evolve; new ideas and tools appear daily. As a result, people who want to remain competitive must keep up with the latest developments in their profession or industry. Online courses allow experienced professionals to refresh their knowledge while managing their job responsibilities easily.

2. *Demonstrate commitment*

Employers often look for candidates who are committed to their field and are willing to invest in their professional development. By earning online certifications, experienced professionals can prove to potential employers that they're dedicated to their success and have the knowledge and skills needed for the job.

3. *Enhance your credibility*

Online certifications can enhance a professional's credibility by demonstrating expertise and mastery of the subject matter. This is an especially important benefit for those looking to advance their careers or switch to new fields. With proper certification, experienced professionals can show potential employers they have the knowledge required for success in any number of roles.

4. *Get recognized*

Earning online certifications gives experienced professionals formal recognition for their work and dedication. In addition, many certifying organizations offer certificates of completion for their courses that a professional can display on resumes, websites, or social media profiles. This recognition can especially benefit experienced professionals seeking to advance into new positions or enhance their reputations.

5. *Benefit from networking opportunities*

Many online certification programs provide networking opportunities through online forums or alums networks. Connecting with other professionals with the same interests and skillset can lead to collaborations, job leads, and career advancement opportunities. Additionally, these connections often help professionals stay updated on industry trends, making them even more valuable in their respective fields.

Overall, earning an online certification provides experienced professionals with numerous benefits. From refreshing knowledge to enhancing credibility and networking opportunities, certifications can help experienced professionals stay ahead of their competition and take control of their career growth.

Technology plays a pivotal role in career progression in today's digital era. It can be used to develop new skills and knowledge sets, build networks of contacts, showcase achievements, and find new opportunities.

However, many professionals need help to make the most of the available technologies. They may need help understanding how to use these tools to their advantage or need more resources or technical expertise.

Therefore, it is important for professionals seeking to progress their careers to learn about the various available technologies and understand how they can be used effectively. This includes researching technology trends and strategically utilizing platforms like LinkedIn or Twitter.

Professionals should focus on learning how to create an effective digital profile, using social media to reach potential employers, and mastering the art of creating a great online portfolio. Additionally, having a sound understanding of how to use analytics and data-driven insights to inform decisions can be a valuable asset in progressing one's career.

Finally, technology can also aid job-seeking activities such as writing targeted resumes and cover letters that use keywords identified through research, developing automated tracking systems for applications sent out, or using software programs to review job postings.

Overall, leveraging technology is essential for managers and leaders to progress in their careers. By understanding the available tools and learning how to use them efficiently, professionals can gain an advantage in their job-seeking activities and professional development.

Strategies for Leveraging Technology in Career Progression

To make the most of technology in career progression, professionals must first understand how to strategically use various tools and platforms. They should also understand how digital profiles, analytics, and data-driven insights can be used to their advantage.

Here are some strategies for leveraging technology in career progression:

1. Research technology trends and identify the best ways to utilize platforms like LinkedIn or Twitter.
2. Create a strong digital profile that showcases your skills, knowledge, and experience.
3. Use social media to reach potential employers—create interesting posts, share relevant news stories or updates about industry developments, connect with other professionals, etc.
4. Master the art of creating a great online portfolio—use visuals and multimedia to showcase your work.
5. Use analytics and data-driven insights to inform decisions about your career progression.
6. Utilise software programs such as Applicant Tracking Systems (ATS) to review job postings.
7. Write targeted resumes and cover letters using researched keywords.
8. Develop automated tracking systems for applications sent out.

By leveraging technology in their career progression, professionals can stay ahead of the competition and create new opportunities for growth and advancement. First, however, they need to understand how these tools can be used effectively to benefit from them fully. With a sound knowledge of the available technologies, managers and leaders can take control of their professional growth and achieve their desired career success.

PART VI

MONETISING THE EXPERIENCE AND BRANCHING OUT AS AN ENTREPRENEUR

TURNING YOUR EXPERTISE INTO A VALUABLE ASSET

It's no secret that experience and expertise are invaluable in the workplace, especially for those in senior management roles. But how do you turn your hard-earned expertise into a valuable asset?

Almost everyone is an authority on something. Many of us have talents and skills that we are more passionate about than our nine-to-five professions, whether you know how to turn canned food into a gourmet cooked meal or you're the person everyone goes to for handyman assistance.

The internet has made it easy to swiftly transform your skills into a reliable source of income, so keep them from being a hobby.

Use the internet in various ways to share your knowledge with others and earn a respectable income. Finding the ideal fit for your personality and industry speciality is simple when many possibilities are available.

First, it's important to assess yourself and your skill set honestly. Ask yourself, "What do I do well? What am I not so good at?"

Once you have identified your strengths and weaknesses, it's time to focus on developing and honing those skills. Consider taking classes or seminars to build your knowledge base and teach you new team management strategies. Additionally, look for opportunities to expand your capabilities by taking on more responsibility or tackling projects outside your comfort zone.

It's also important to identify the areas where you need support from other people or departments. Don't be afraid to reach out and make connections with colleagues who can help you grow professionally.

Showing initiative is one of the best ways to demonstrate your value as a leader—something that will become increasingly important when progressing in your career.

Ensure you stay current on the latest trends and technologies in your field. This will ensure you stay ahead of the curve and maintain relevance with rapidly evolving industries.

It's important to recognize that experience doesn't always equate to a successful career trajectory; it's about continuing to grow and develop as an individual passionate about their profession. Leverage your skills, knowledge, and expertise to make the most of everything you do. With these strategies and tips in mind, you'll be on track for a successful career.

18   DEVELOPING A SIDE HUSTLE TO GENERATE ADDITIONAL INCOME

Today, many professionals find themselves stuck in a career rut. They may have years of experience but feel their careers stagnate and go nowhere. One way to overcome this roadblock is by developing a side hustle to generate additional income. This can provide the financial freedom needed to pursue other avenues of career growth or even leave your current job and take up a new role.

Before beginning your side hustle journey, it's important first to identify what type of business activity you want to pursue. For example, do you want to start an online store selling items such as handmade crafts? Or launch an app development firm? Then, once you've identified the avenue for your side hustle, research how to make it successful.

Look into potential customers, suppliers, and collaborators for your side hustle. Watch for industry trends and emerging technologies that could help you reach more people. Network regularly with other professionals in a similar situation as yourself who can offer valuable advice on overcoming any career roadblocks you're facing.

Before launching your business, ensure that all legal requirements, such as registering the business name and obtaining permissions from your employer, licenses or permits, have been fulfilled. In addition, have a clear understanding of the taxes applicable to your side hustle and save money along the way so you can pay them when they are due.

Remember, it can take time before your side gig starts generating income, so manage your expectations and take things one step at a time. With hard work, dedication, and persistence, you'll be able to reap the rewards of your efforts soon enough.

By focusing on developing a side hustle, you can take control of your career progression and generate additional income. In addition, the right strategy and mindset could open up many opportunities to pursue new roles or even launch your own business. So, get out there and start making your dreams a reality!

19   IDENTIFYING OPPORTUNITIES TO MONETIZE YOUR KNOWLEDGE

As a manager or leader with many years of experience, you are in a unique position to monetize your knowledge. This can include offering consulting services to other businesses or giving lectures and seminars on topics related to your expertise.

To take advantage of this opportunity, it is important to identify the services you could offer as a consultant or a speaker. Consider both external opportunities (such as conference speaking engagements) and internal opportunities (providing advice within your organization). Once you have identified these potential avenues for monetization, investigate networking events where you could meet potential clients and partners.

When developing these relationships, it is important to assess the needs of your audience. Not only will this help you determine what services you can offer, but it will also give you insight into how your clients think and operate. This knowledge can be invaluable in helping you progress in your career.

In addition, look for ways to increase the value of your service offering. For example, consider developing a portfolio of case studies showcasing successful projects or creating a blog or podcast on topics related to your expertise. Doing so will demonstrate that you are an authority on the subject matter and help draw potential customers to your business.

Assessing the Needs of Prospective Clients

When assessing the needs of prospective clients, it is important to consider the current market trends and technologies. Doing so will help you determine which services are currently in demand and what expertise you can offer. In addition, consider researching industry publications, attending networking events, and talking to potential customers to understand their needs.

Additionally, assess your skillset and experience. Determine what services you can offer that no one else does and any areas where you have gaps in knowledge or expertise. Seek mentors or attend educational courses to help fill those gaps if necessary.

These measures will enable you to provide a more comprehensive range of services that can add greater value for your clients.

By properly assessing potential customers' needs, you can better position yourself as an expert in your field and effectively monetize your knowledge. Doing so will help you progress in your career and provide a valuable service to others.

Maximising Your Professional Success

Finally, it is important to ensure that you maximize your professional success both within and outside your current job. To do this, focus on developing long-term relationships with colleagues and clients. Keep up-to-date with industry trends and technologies, attend networking events, and pitch ideas demonstrating how to add value for employers or business partners.

Creating a portfolio showcasing your work and the results you have achieved is also important. Doing so will demonstrate your expertise to potential employers or business partners, which can help progress your career.

For some professionals, becoming an entrepreneur is the most effective way to progress in their careers. Although this can be risky and daunting, it can provide great rewards if successful.

At the very least, exploring entrepreneurial ventures will help you develop valuable skills that can benefit your career even if you don't pursue it further. These include problem-solving abilities, resilience in adversity, and a better understanding of finance and business strategy.

If you decide to plunge into entrepreneurship, you should thoroughly research the market before launching a venture. This means researching potential competitors and developing a detailed business plan and financial forecast considering potential risks. Identifying the resources and support needed to ensure success is also essential.

Finally, it's important to note that starting a business typically requires long hours and hard work—often with no guarantee of financial or career rewards. However, for some professionals, this is an opportunity to create something entirely new and reap the rewards of their efforts.

Exploring Entrepreneurial Ventures

No matter what career direction, entrepreneurial ventures can be a great way to progress professionally and succeed on your terms. With the right tools and resources, you can use your existing skills and knowledge to create something special - and potentially reap the rewards.

21 BUILDING AN ONLINE PRESENCE

In today's digital age, an online presence is essential for career success. Developing a professional website or blog, creating a profile on LinkedIn, and being active on social media can help you showcase your experience and skills to potential employers. You can also use these platforms to stay informed about the latest trends in your industry and find new opportunities for advancement.

It would be best if you also considered writing articles or contributing content related to your expertise. This will demonstrate your knowledge while allowing you to network with other industry professionals. Furthermore, having an online presence can be helpful when it comes to getting the right connections, as many hiring managers prefer candidates who have taken the initiative by promoting their work ethic through social media outlets.

Finally, having an online presence can also be beneficial when building your brand. Creating content that reflects your values and objectives allows you to stand out from the competition and establish yourself as a leader in your field.

By following these steps and capitalizing on the power of technology, you will enhance your career prospects and become more visible within your chosen industry. Although it may take time to build up followers and create a reliable network of contacts, these efforts will pay off in the long run by helping you progress in your career faster.

How to Set Up Your Online Presence?

Here are some tips on setting up and maintaining a successful online presence:

Build a Professional Website

Every business requires a website. If you don't already have one, you can easily create one or hire someone. First, you will require a domain name, but your first choice might already be taken. But don't worry; many businesses offer domain names, and most are relatively inexpensive.

It's not required that your domain name corresponds to the name of your business. Use keywords that describe your company instead. Consider the keywords that customers might use to find a company like yours.

Retain and Target Customers on Social Media

Social media is a powerful tool for marketing and advertising your business. Platforms such as Facebook, Twitter, and Instagram are popular choices for companies. Ensure you post content regularly so your customers can learn about the latest products and services.

Content is King

Writing articles, blog posts, or creating content related to your field of expertise effectively showcases what makes you different from other professionals in the same industry. You can also use this platform to network with other professionals in the same field by commenting and engaging with their work. This will help create relationships that benefit both parties in the future.

Make Connections

An online presence can allow you to connect with people who can help you progress in your career. Use social media platforms such as LinkedIn and Twitter to find contacts that could lead to new job opportunities. You should also consider attending events related to your expertise or participating in webinars/online conferences that can help you make more connections.

Develop a Personal Brand

Having an online presence is beneficial for networking and can be used to showcase your values and objectives, making you stand out from other professionals in the same field. However, developing a personal brand requires consistency so that all content reflects the desired message.

By following these steps, you can build an effective online presence to help you progress in your career faster.

22 FINDING FUNDING FOR YOUR BUSINESS IDEAS

For many experienced managers and leaders, an important roadblock to progressing their careers is finding the capital to turn their ideas into reality. Whether it's launching a new product or service, starting a business, expanding a current project, or taking advantage of an untapped market opportunity, often, funding can be hard to come by.

Fortunately, in some ways, experienced professionals can access capital and support for their projects. Here are some tips on how to make the most of your knowledge, expertise, and resources when looking for funding:

Begin with Bootstrapping

Many business owners employ "bootstrapping," which refers to financing your firm using any personal funds you can obtain while they are first starting. Your savings account, credit cards, and any home equity lines of credit are often included.

Using the money you already have instead of borrowing or raising it is a fantastic strategy in many situations; in fact, several entrepreneurs continue to bootstrap their businesses until they become successful. This can be advantageous because you will only have large loans and ongoing obligations that weigh you down, especially if you encounter roadblocks.

But, bringing in outside sources of money may be useful if you want to grow your business swiftly. So, what occurs when your money runs out or you need fmore? There are several typical areas to start, but ultimately, it will depend on the type of business you're developing.

Consider Friends and Family

It may feel unsafe to ask your friends and family for money, but reaching out to your loved ones is frequently a wise first move before seeking outside assistance. Also, it always helps to inquire. Although Aunt Irene definitely won't be able to afford your new social network for dog owners, she might be moved to give you a few thousand dollars to get things started.

But preparing a business strategy before approaching your friends and family for financial support would be best. You should ensure that fully understand what you're offering by explaining things like what you want to charge, how you plan to make money, and whether you're requesting a loan, an investment, or a gift. You should make these things clear before asking for funding.

Explore Alternative Funding Sources

Many micro-loan companies lend to start-ups and entrepreneurs if you seek a relatively modest amount (between $25 and $5,000). Examples include Kiva and Accion. These websites offer services to low-income American business owners or non-profit organizations (some only provide micro-loans to those living below the poverty line). But, if you believe you could be eligible, visit their websites for more details.

Another option is the increasingly well-liked crowd-funding websites, like IndieGoGo and Kickstarter, which give you a platform to raise money from tiny, local supporters online. You'll establish benefits for donors who pledge a particular amount of money, set up a campaign, and specify a goal amount of money you want to raise. Then, you raise money for the campaign over a predetermined time frame.

With Kickstarter, you can only keep the money if you reach your entire fundraising target, but with IndieGoGo, you can keep any amount you raise.

Look Local

You should check out your local small business development centre if you're starting a small business rather than a tech start-up you hope will become the next Facebook. The Small Business Administration (SBA) alone has 63 centres nationwide, and many institutions have a centre.

These organizations can not only help you connect with business networking groups and angel investors for funding, but they can also help you identify the kinds of loans and funding you could be eligible for and assist you in applying.

Your local chamber of commerce is also a gold mine of knowledge and direction regarding where to find regional funding. Numerous big cities have initiatives and groups that aim to boost local commerce.

Consider Taking Out Loans

You may be eligible for a conventional bank loan if you demonstrate that you've begun to develop traction and make money (and that a loan would help you earn even more). In addition, numerous financial institutions and Government schemes have declared a stronger commitment to small businesses.

Look to Angels

If you're starting a tech business, you'll likely require more financing in the long run than bootstrapping, and crowd-funding will allow you to hire staff or secure office space. As a result, you'll likely need to contact outside investors. Angel investors are an excellent place to start because they are frequently seasoned businessmen with high net worths seeking to invest in new startups. A typical angel investment ranges from $10,000 to several million dollars.

Venturing Into Bigger Capital

Venture capital for significant finance (at least $1 million) is best. This is because venture capitalists (VCs) are more likely to demand a thorough and complete business plan, but they also can provide you with bigger sums of cash.

VCs generally make several investments on behalf of their clients, hoping that one (or more) of them would be profitable enough to recoup their clients' initial contributions. They see all kinds of businesses, so you must make yours stand out to succeed. Also, you should be aware that VCs typically expect a return of between three and ten times their initial investment within the next five to seven years. So, it's important to have an exit strategy in mind.

After you've decided to ask for VC funding, it's time to use your contacts (and their networks) to see whom you can talk to. The easiest approach to getting meetings with VCs is through introductions from other investors or entrepreneurs. Lacking any contacts? You can also search the National Venture Capital Association website and pitch your company to the investors you contact, albeit doing so is riskier. Although dialling a venture investor on the phone may be challenging, it is a place to start

PART VII

CONCLUSION

23 REFLECTION ON CAREER PROGRESSION STRATEGIES

As experienced managers and leaders, reflecting on our career progression strategies is important. Taking time to pause and examine the successes and failures in our professional lives can help us identify patterns, gain insight into what has worked or not, and ultimately, inform more successful choices in the future.

The first step to reflection is to consider the accomplishments that have shaped your career so far. For example, think about times when you successfully navigated a challenging situation at work, made valuable contributions, or took ownership of an initiative with positive results. Even if the impact was small, reflecting on these moments of success can motivate future work efforts.

Another helpful strategy is to analyze areas where you feel stuck or frustrated in your job. Think about the outcomes you have been aiming for and how these might be related to your current career roadblocks. For example, it could be that there is a skill or task you need to develop from taking on new responsibilities or that it is time to shift focus onto an area of your professional life that has been neglected.

Consider the skills, knowledge, and expertise you bring to your job. Take stock of what makes you unique and determine what differentiates you from other professionals in similar roles. A clear understanding of your strengths and weaknesses can guide decision-making around career progression and ensure that the steps in this process are relevant and beneficial.

By reflecting on our successes and failures, understanding areas where we feel stuck, and identifying our unique skills, knowledge, and expertise, we can develop more effective strategies to manage career progression. This will help us take control of our professional growth and make the most of our experiences.

By understanding these aspects of ourselves, we can devise a plan tailored to our needs—one that considers current circumstances and future aspirations. With this insight, even experienced managers and leaders can set themselves up for career success.

24 FREQUENTLY ASKED QUESTIONS AND FINAL THOUGHTS

This section answers some questions that experienced managers and leaders often ask regarding their career progression:

Q1:   What are the most common roadblocks to career success?

A1:   Some of the most common roadblocks to career success include clarity about what you want to achieve, inadequate networking skills, little self-promotion, stalled job search efforts, and too much focus on perfectionism. It is important to identify these roadblocks before they become too difficult to overcome.

Q2:   How can I make sure that my current job counts towards my long-term goals?

A2:   To ensure your current job counts towards your long-term goals, it is helpful to create a career plan that outlines what you want to achieve in the future and develop strategies for using your current job. It is also important to be proactive about networking with people with similar goals and interests and look for opportunities within your job that will help build your skills and experience.

Q3:   How can I make sure I remain competitive in my field?

A3:   To remain competitive in your field, it is essential to stay up-to-date on industry trends, attend conferences and seminars related to your profession, network with other professionals in the same industry, and take advantage of learning opportunities. Additionally, it's important to focus on developing soft skills, such as communication and problem-solving, essential for success in the modern workplace.

Finally, it is important to remember that career progression can sometimes be slow, but you can achieve your goals with commitment and hard work. Focus on developing a plan of action and staying motivated to reach your ultimate career objectives.